worksheets, activities, and reflections for grades 6–12

STUDY GUIDE

T0170676

FIGHTER IN VELVET GLOVES

Alaska Civil Rights Hero
Elizabeth Peratrovich

SNOWY
OWL
BOOKS

University of Alaska Press, Fairbanks

Text © 2021 University of Alaska Press

Published by
University of Alaska Press
P.O. Box 756240
Fairbanks, AK 99775-6240

Cover and interior design by UA Press.

Cover image Elizabeth Peratrovich, *We Can Do It,* acrylic on canvas by
Apayo Moore, 2014. www.apayoart.com.

Unit Foundation Standards by Rebecca Stenson, Alaskan educator and curriculum specialist.

Library of Congress Cataloging-in-Publication Data
Names: Boochever, Annie, author.
Title: Fighter in Velvet Gloves: Student/Teacher Study Guide / Annie
    Boochever.
Description: Fairbanks, AK : University of Alaska Press, 2021. | At head
    of title: "A true story for young teens; Alaska civil rights hero
    Elizabeth Peratrovich" | Audience: Ages 10–16 | Audience: Grades 6-9
Identifiers: LCCN 2020030593 (print) | LCCN 2020030594 (ebook) | ISBN
    9781602234451 (paperback) | ISBN 9781602234468 (ebook)
Subjects: LCSH: Boochever, Annie. Fighter in Velvet Gloves. | Peratrovich,
    Elizabeth, 1911-1958–Juvenile literature. | Tlingit
    Indians–Alaska–Study and teaching (Secondary) | Indians of North
    America–Civil rights Study and teaching (Secondary)
Classification: LCC E99.T6 B667 2021 (print) | LCC E99.T6 (ebook) | DDC
    970.004/97–dc23
LC record available at https://lccn.loc.gov/2020030593
LC ebook record available at https://lccn.loc.gov/2020030594

This book is dedicated to the
Alaska Native Sisterhood and Alaska Native Brotherhood
for nearly a century of tireless work on behalf of
Alaska Native people and toward a better Alaska for all.

Table of Contents

Fighter in Velvet Gloves
Alaska Civil Rights Hero Elizabeth Peratrovich vii

PRE-READING ACTIVITIES

Preview the Book 3

Vocabulary 5

KWL Chart. 7

STUDENT RESPONSE

Introduction, Prologue, Chapter 1 11

Chapters 2 and 3 13

Chapters 4 and 5 15

Chapters 6, 7, and 8 17

Chapters 9–12. 19

Chapters 13–16. 21

Epilogue and Afterward 25

FINAL REFLECTION

Learning Outcomes 29

KWL Chart. 31

Essay on Racism. 33

Alaska Locations 35

TEACHER'S GUIDE: REFERENCES

Unit Foundation Standards 39

Vocabulary 43

Map Key 45

TEACHER'S GUIDE: RESPONSES

Introduction, Prologue, Chapter 1 49

Chapters 2 and 3 51

Chapters 4 and 5 53

Chapters 6, 7, and 8 55

Chapters 9–12. 57

Chapters 13–16. 59

Epilogue and Afterward 61

About the Author: Annie Boochever 63

About the Son: Roy Peratrovich Jr. 64

Fighter in Velvet Gloves
Alaska Civil Rights Hero Elizabeth Peratrovich

"NO NATIVES ALLOWED!" blared the store-front sign at the young Tlingit Indian girl. The sting of those words would stay with Elizabeth Peratrovich all her life.

They would also make her determined to work for change. Years later, as a seasoned fighter for equality, she would deliver her own eloquent message—one that helped change Alaska and the nation forever. Written in collaboration with Elizabeth's eldest son and only living child, Roy Peratrovich Jr., *Fighter in Velvet Gloves* tells the life story of this inspirational Alaskan and American hero, for readers 10 and up.

Elizabeth was born in Petersburg, Alaska, on an auspicious date, July 4, 1911. But the circumstances surrounding her birth were veiled in secrecy and shame. Nevertheless, Elizabeth grew up with her adopted parents, Tlingit couple Andrew and Jean Wanamaker, who showered her with great love and affection and raised her in the Alaska Native way. She traveled with her father, a lay Presbyterian Minister, in the boat he helped build while a student at the Sheldon Jackson Boarding School for Alaska Natives, up and down the coast of Southeast Alaska. She sat in the back of the churches, legs dangling,

Elizabeth Peratrovich. *Photo courtesy of the Peratrovich Family photo collection*

listening intently to every word. She learned later that if she chose her words carefully, as her dad did, people paid attention. She could not have known that she would revisit those same small towns years later as one of the greatest speakers of her generation, preaching about civil rights.

Married in 1931 to Tlingit leader Roy Peratrovich Sr., Elizabeth and Roy Sr. worked as a team with many others to overcome blatant "Jim Crow" racism, endemic throughout Alaska in the thirties and forties. Elizabeth recognized at a young age that Alaska Native people were separated in many ways, with the nicest places reserved for the white people. Restaurants, stores, schools, and even cemeteries were segregated. The Peratroviches wanted a better life for their children, one where they were not barred entrance because of their race.

In 1945, when Elizabeth was thirty-four years old, she met with the Territorial Governor Ernest Gruening, who was sympathetic to the Alaska Natives' battle for equal rights. They agreed that Elizabeth needed to travel throughout Alaska to garner support for the anti-discrimination bill that would be voted on in the next session of the Territorial Legislature. But, of course, there was no such thing as government funding for such an undertaking. She had three children and a husband with no flexibility in his job. How could she do it? Then, as now, no roads connected most southeast Alaska towns. The only way to travel was by plane.

Luckily, she found Alaska Coastal Airline pilot and owner Shell Simmons, who graciously offered to fly Elizabeth in his Grumann Goose whenever there was an extra seat.

But lack of affordable daycare left her with few options for her children. A friend, Minnie Field, ran an orphanage about 16 miles north of Juneau. Minnie took the two oldest in for the summer. Little four-year-old Lori was small enough to ride on her mother's lap. Shell flew them to every town hall and school gym on his route. Would all her work pay off?

The answer came on February 5, 1945. In front of an all-white, male senatorial body, Elizabeth spoke with eloquence and grace about the evils of racism. Her powerful and

GUIDE OVERVIEW

Subject Area Reading, English, Language Arts, Geography, History/Social Studies

Grade Level Grades 6-12

Approximate Time Needed 3-4 weeks

Prerequisite Skills Reading, writing, speaking, listening, working collaboratively

Unit Vocabulary Glossary of terms

National Common CORE, Alaska State Standards, Alaska Culturally Responsive Schools See Appendix D for referenced standards

carefully chosen words crowned years of work by Alaska Native people and their allies. Alaska's landmark Anti-Discrimination Act passed, nearly two decades before President Lyndon Johnson signed the U.S. Civil Rights Act of 1964.

Today Alaskans honor Elizabeth Peratrovich (1911-1958) every year on February 16, "For her courageous, unceasing efforts to eliminate discrimination and bring about equal rights in Alaska" (Alaska Statutes 44.12.065). In 2020 the U.S. Mint released a commemorative one-dollar coin graced with Elizabeth Peratrovich's image, honoring the Peratrovich family, the Tlingit Nation, Alaska Native people, and indeed, all Native Americans.

PRE-READING ACTIVITIES

Preview the Book

NAME: _____   DATE: _____

Before you begin the novel, take time to look over the cover. Read the title, the author's name, and her collaborator's. Look at the picture on the front. What do you think this story will be about? Where do you think it takes place? Jot down some of your ideas below.

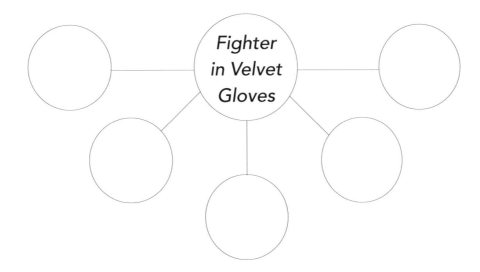

Fighter in Velvet Gloves

Now read the back of the book. What does that tell you?
What were the main issues Elizabeth dealt with in her life? List three of them below.

1. _____
2. _____
3. _____

DIRECT YOUR READING

Fighter in Velvet Gloves is all about overcoming seemingly unsurmountable challenges.
In small groups, talk about one or two big challenges or obstacles you have met with in your life:

      How did you handle them?

      Have you experienced racism or discrimination?

      Have you witnessed it? How did you respond?

Vocabulary

NAME: _____   DATE: _____

Aboriginal	Moiety
Assimilate	Prejudice
Civil Rights	Racism
Clan	Regalia
Discrimination	Segregation
Grumman Goose	Senate
House of Representatives	State
Indigenous	Subsistence
Inequity	Territory
Iñupiaq	Testimony
Ku.éex'	Tlingit
Legislature	Tuberculosis
Mixed breed	Unanimous

KWL Chart: Know, Want, Learn

NAME: _____   DATE: _____

What do you already know about Alaska? About Alaska Native people? About racism in Alaska? About Elizabeth Peratrovich? These are the kinds of things you can put in your KWL Chart. As you read the book, you can add to the last column.

What I KNOW	What I WANT to Know	What I LEARNED

STUDENT RESPONSE

Introduction, Prologue, Chapter 1

NAME: _____   DATE: _____

PERSONAL REFLECTION

(Answer on separate paper or use for classroom discussion.)

What do you know about adoption? Today, most adoptions are "open," meaning the identity of the birth parents are disclosed and families are often in contact with one another. This was not the case in the early 20th century. Which kind of adoption would you prefer and why? How might Elizabeth's life have been different if her adoption had been open? Write your ideas down in one or two paragraphs.

SHORT ANSWER

1. Describe in your own words how the introduction sets the stage for Elizabeth's story.

_____

_____

_____

2. Who wrote the prologue? What purpose does it serve in advancing the story of Elizabeth?

_____

_____

_____

3. How did the prologue better inform the reader about the metaphor "Fighter in Velvet Gloves?" What does that metaphor suggest about Elizabeth? As you read the book, note if the metaphor is repeated.

_____

_____

4. In the first chapter, the reader learns about the circumstances surrounding Elizabeth's birth. This is the first time this information has been publicly revealed. Why is it important to include details of her birth in the story of Elizabeth's life?

5. See what you can find out about the history of tuberculosis in Alaska Native or Native American communities. Write a couple of paragraphs about what you learned and how it pertains to this book.

CRITICAL THINKING (Answer on separate paper or use for classroom discussion.)

How does the first paragraph in the introduction make you feel? Why?

Why do you think the place names in the first chapter and throughout the book are spelled first in Tlingit and then translated into English?

Chapters 2 and 3

NAME: _____   DATE: _____

PERSONAL REFLECTION

(Answer on separate paper or use for classroom discussion.)

Why didn't Elizabeth's family depend on grocery stores? What do you know about living a "subsistence lifestyle"? How common is it in Alaska today? Do you or your family practice any kind of subsistence? Have you ever eaten any of the foods discussed in this chapter? Do you think Alaska Native people continue to be separated from non-Natives in Alaska today? Please explain.

SHORT ANSWER

1. Why was public speaking so important to Alaska Native people?
Is it as important today as when Elizabeth was growing up?

_____

_____

_____

2. Describe the Alaska Native Brotherhood and Sisterhood.
Why were they so important? What do you hear about them today?

_____

_____

_____

3. On page 10, Sheldon Jackson's approach to education was called "misguided." Describe his goals for his students and comment on why they might have been "misguided."

4. What events in Elizabeth's life do you think helped her become an effective public speaker?

CRITICAL THINKING

(Answer on separate paper or use for classroom discussion.)

What can you find out about the "boarding school" experience for Native Americans outside Alaska? Check the Bibliography for sources. Extra reading: *My Name is Not Easy* by Debby Dahl Edwardson, finalist for the National Book Award, and a true story about the Alaska Native boarding school experience.

Can you see any positives from the boarding school experience? What were the negatives? Would you want to go to a boarding school like the one Elizabeth or Roy Sr. attended? Why or why not?

Elizabeth's high school graduation. *Photo courtesy of the Peratrovich Family photo collection*

Chapters 4 and 5

RESPONSE

NAME: _____   DATE: _____

PERSONAL REFLECTION
(Answer on separate paper or use for classroom discussion.)

In chapter 3, we learn about the Indian Citizenship Act of 1924. Did it surprise you that prior to 1924, Native Americans were not considered U.S. citizens? How do you think that affected the way Alaska Natives and Native Americans were treated by the government? How do you think your life would be different if you were not treated like an American citizen even though you were born in the U.S.? Can you think of a similar situation today that applies to immigrants?

SHORT ANSWER

1. On page 15, we read that the Ketchikan High School was not segregated because of a lawsuit by William Paul Sr. Cite some other important things William Paul Sr. did for Alaska Natives.

_____

_____

_____

2. What happened to Roy and Elizabeth Peratrovich's dream of becoming teachers?

_____

_____

_____

3. Why did Elizabeth want to move from Klawock to Juneau?

4. Can you name at least one U.S. Territory that exists today?
What is the difference between a state and a territory?
Describe the 1st and 2nd Organic Acts.

CRITICAL THINKING
(Answer on separate paper or use for classroom discussion.)

Although statehood is not discussed in the book, Governor Gruening was a champion for the cause. Statehood transformed Alaska. Research some of the arguments for and against Alaska becoming a state. See if you can find out what Alaskans think about statehood today. Do Alaska Natives have a different opinion about statehood from non-Native Alaska residents?

PROS	CONS

Chapters 6, 7, and 8

RESPONSE

NAME: _____   DATE: _____

PERSONAL REFLECTION

(Answer on separate paper or use for classroom discussion.)

If you were not allowed to go to the school of your choice, how would you feel? What would you do about it? How do you think the Alaska Native students who attended the government schools felt? Can you find historic examples of segregated schools in the rest of the United States? How were they similar or different from Alaska's segregated schools? Are there segregated schools today? How are they different or similar?

Alaska Native people volunteered for military duty during WWII in large numbers. Why do you think they weren't allowed to vote? Are our voting laws better today? Are there still areas where it is difficult to vote? Explain.

SHORT ANSWER

1. In the early twentieth century, why did many Alaska Natives speak not only Tlingit and English but also Russian?

_____

_____

_____

2. Why was Territorial Governor Ernest Gruening sympathetic to the anti-discrimination bill? What did he do to try to ease relations between Alaska Native people and non-Natives?

_____

_____

_____

3. Who appointed Gruening to be the Territorial Governor of Alaska in 1939?

4. Why didn't the anti-discrimination bill pass in 1943?

5. Who was Alberta Schenk?
How did her actions affect support for the anti-discrimination bill?

6. Name three things Elizabeth stressed in her travels to gain support for the anti-discrimination bill.

7. What was "the Toilet Paper Defense"?

CRITICAL THINKING
(Answer on separate paper or use for classroom discussion.)

If Elizabeth were alive today and working on the same issues, do you think the challenges would be easier with social media? Why? Write about a few of the advantages and disadvantages. Have you ever seen racism on social media? Explain.

Chapters 9–12

NAME: _____   DATE: _____

PERSONAL REFLECTION

(Answer on separate paper or use for classroom discussion.)

Finding day care is an age-old problem, especially for women. Lack of day care may well have led to Elizabeth's adoption, and it nearly prevented her from doing the work necessary to gain support for the anti-discrimination bill. Do you remember attending a day care program as a young child? See if you can find out what day care for a child typically costs today. When Elizabeth needed day care, there wasn't any. What did you think about her solution? How big of a problem is this for our country? Research and write about some of the impacts childcare, or lack of it, has on our society. Brainstorm some solutions.

SHORT ANSWER

1. Who were the new legislators that ran and won as a result of Elizabeth's travels? Where were they from? Why was their election significant?

_____

_____

2. Who was Shell Simmons? Why was he so integral to the success of the anti-discrimination bill? Research in the glossary why he was such an important figure in Alaska aviation.

_____

_____

_____

Elizabeth and her
adoptive mother
Jean Wanamaker
circa 1919.
*Photo courtesy of the
Peratrovich Family
photo collection*

CRITICAL THINKING

(Answer on separate paper or use for classroom discussion.)

How did Elizabeth's discovery of her birth mother affect her? Did you think Reverend
Soboleff was right to tell her? Why?

What do you like the best about Elizabeth's story so far? Why?

RESPONSE

NAME: _____   DATE: _____

PERSONAL REFLECTION
(Answer on separate paper or use for classroom discussion.)

Why do you think the author included a description of the weather on the day Elizabeth delivered her testimony?

Once again childcare was an issue for Elizabeth on the day she was to deliver her planned testimony. What do you think of her solution?

SHORT ANSWER

1. The bill passed easily in the House. Why was the bill less likely to pass in the Senate?

_____

_____

2. List some of the senators who supported the anti-discrimination bill.

_____

_____

3. List at least three senators who opposed the bill and state their reasons.

_____

_____

4. Describe Roy Peratrovich Sr.'s testimony.

5. What was the final vote tally in the Senate? In the House?

6. What did Governor Gruening say to Elizabeth right after he signed the bill?

7. What was so special about the Peratroviches' celebration at the Baranof Hotel?

8. Describe at least two other things Elizabeth Peratrovich did to improve the lives of Alaska Natives after the anti-discrimination bill passed.

9. On page 61, the author describes Elizabeth's fundamental belief that "the greatest barrier to equality is ignorance." What do you think this means?

10. Describe an issue that you care strongly about that you could imagine giving a speech about.

11. On page 65, there is a quote by Elizabeth Peratrovich that explains why she thinks it is impossible to discriminate against someone who feels no inferiority. What does she mean by that?

12. Why do you think Elizabeth chose to die in the Christian Science Care Facility in Seattle?

13. How old was Elizabeth when she died?

CRITICAL THINKING
(Answer on separate paper or use for classroom discussion.)

What do you think about Elizabeth's question to the senators about laws not preventing crimes?

In Elizabeth's testimony, she mentions three kinds of persons who practice discrimination against the "Indians" and other "Native people." Describe those three kinds of people in your own words. Do you recognize any of the descriptions as people you know today? Please explain.

There are several quotations by Elizabeth Peratrovich in the book. Pick one and write it here. Explain why you chose that particular quote and what it means to you.

Epilogue and Afterword

RESPONSE

NAME: _____   DATE: _____

PERSONAL REFLECTION
(Answer on separate paper or use for classroom discussion.)

Does Alaska have any other celebrated civil rights heroes like Elizabeth Peratrovich that you know of? Can you write about another Alaska civil rights hero who is a national figure?

Although Elizabeth Peratrovich is gaining fame on the national scene, she is still relatively unknown outside Alaska. Why do you think that is?

SHORT ANSWER

1. What day is Elizabeth Peratrovich Day in Alaska, and when was that day made official? Who signed the Executive Proclamation?

_____

_____

2. Name at least three physical monuments honoring Elizabeth Peratrovich.

_____

_____

3. Describe the latest honor by the U.S. Mint.

_____

_____

25

4. Where are Elizabeth and Roy Peratrovich Sr. buried?

_____

_____

_____

5. In the Epilogue, the author cites her many connections to Elizabeth and those involved in passage of the anti-discrimination bill she discovered while writing and researching the book. Did this help to strengthen the author's credibility? Please explain your answer.

_____

_____

_____

6. How did the epilogue section make you think about the rest of the book?

_____

_____

_____

PERSONAL REFLECTION

(Answer on separate paper or use for classroom discussion.)

Suggested further reading: in this case, instead of reading, watch the PBS Documentary _For the Rights of All: Ending Jim Crow in Alaska_.

Elizabeth could never have achieved passage of the anti-discrimination bill by herself. Write about other individuals or organizations that helped her.

Did the anti-discrimination bill make prejudice go away? Describe an incident you have personally witnessed involving racism or discrimination. Are there other kinds of discrimination besides racism? Name some.

What can you personally do to help eliminate racism and discrimination?

FINAL REFLECTION

Learning Outcomes

NAME: _____   DATE: _____

Go back and complete your KWL Chart. Share with a partner.
Write one thing that surprised you about your partner's chart.

_____

_____

Did you like the book *Fighter in Velvet Gloves*?
Why or why not? Cite at least five reasons for your answer.

_____

_____

_____

_____

_____

_____

If you were writing the book, what would you have done differently?

_____

_____

_____

_____

KWL Chart: Know, Want, Learn

NAME: _____   DATE: _____

What I KNOW	What I WANT to Know	What I LEARNED

Essay on Racism

REFLECTION

NAME: _____   DATE: _____

You don't have to look far to find examples of racism in the world both historically and currently. Pick one and write a short 1-2 page essay about how it connects to something in your life.

Alaska Locations

NAME: _____   DATE: _____

All of these places were mentioned in the book. See if you can find them on the map.

Kichxáan (Ketchikan)   Deering
Juneau   Aleutian Islands
Lawáak (Klawock)   Kéix' (Kake)
Gánti Yaakw Séedi (Petersburg)   Tinaghu (Tenakee)
Deishú (Haines)   Sheet'ká (Sitka)
Wales   Maaxłakxaała (Metlakatla)
Nome

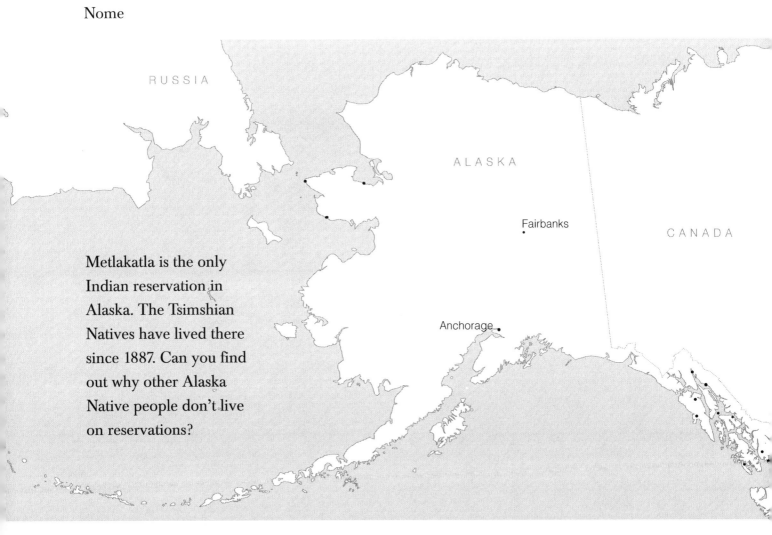

Metlakatla is the only Indian reservation in Alaska. The Tsimshian Natives have lived there since 1887. Can you find out why other Alaska Native people don't live on reservations?

TEACHER'S GUIDE
REFERENCES

Unit Foundation Standards

The standards referenced below are Common Core State Standards and Alaska State Standards for English Language Arts, which are identical unless otherwise noted. Also included are curriculum standards for the Alaska State Standards for Culturally Responsive Schools. Grade 7 standards are listed as a reference. Please keep in mind that upper grades will fall within the same standard but with increasing complexity, and conversely, standards for lower grades will demonstrate decreasing complexity. Please refer to your specific grade level.

STANDARDS ABBREVIATIONS

C=Cultural; L=Language; RI=Reading: Informational Text; RH=Reading: History/Social Studies; SL=Speaking and Listening; W=Writing; WHST=Writing: History, Social Studies, Science, & Technical Subjects

RI.7.1 Cite several pieces of textual evidence to support analysis of what the text says explicitly as well as inferences drawn from the text.

RI.7.3 Analyze the interactions between individuals, events, and ideas in a text (e.g., how ideas influence individuals or events, or how individuals influence ideas or events).

RI.7.4 Determine the meaning of words and phrases as they are used in a text, including figurative, connotative, and technical meanings; analyze the impact of a specific word choice on meaning and tone.

RI.7.5 Analyze the structure an author uses to organize a text, including how the major sections contribute to the whole and to the development of the ideas.

RI.7.6 Determine an author's point of view or purpose in a text and analyze how the author distinguishes his or her position from that of others. (Alaska State Standards uses slightly different language but still covers the same material.)

RI.7.10 By the end of the year, read and comprehend literary nonfiction, within a complexity band appropriate to grade 7 (from upper grade 6 to grade 8), with scaffolding as needed at the high end of the range. (Same language for grades 9-12.)

W.7.1 Write arguments to support claims with clear reasons and relevant evidence.

W.7.2 Write informative/explanatory texts to examine a topic and convey ideas, concepts, and information through the selection, organization, and analysis of relevant content.

W.7.4 Produce clear and coherent writing in which the development, organization, and style are appropriate to task, purpose, and audience.

W.7.7 Conduct short research projects to answer a question, drawing on several sources and generating additional related, focused questions for further research and investigation.

W.7.9 Draw evidence from literary or informational texts to support analysis, reflection, and research.

SL.7.1 Engage effectively in a range of collaborative discussions (one-on-one, in groups, and teacher-led) with diverse partners on grade 7 topics, texts, and issues, building on others' ideas and expressing their own clearly.

SL7.4 Present claims and findings, emphasizing salient points in a focused, coherent manner with pertinent descriptions, facts, details, and examples; use appropriate eye contact, adequate volume, and clear pronunciation.

L.7.1 Demonstrate command of the conventions of standard English grammar and usage when writing or speaking.

L.7.2 Demonstrate command of the conventions of standard English capitalization, punctuation, and spelling when writing.

L.7.3 Use knowledge of language and its conventions when writing, speaking, reading, or listening.

L.7.4 Determine or clarify the meaning of unknown and multiple-meaning words and phrases based on grade 7 reading and content, choosing flexibly from a range of strategies.

L.7.5 Demonstrate understanding of figurative language, word relationships, and nuances in word meanings.

RH.6-8.1 Cite specific textual evidence to support analysis of primary and secondary sources.

RH.6-8.4 Determine the meaning of words and phrases as they are used in a text, including vocabulary specific to domains related to history/social studies.

WHST.6-8.1 Write arguments focused on discipline-specific content.

WHST.6-8.2 Write informative/explanatory texts, including the narration of historical events, scientific procedures/ experiments, or technical processes.

WHST.6-8.4 Produce clear and coherent writing in which the development, organization, and style are appropriate to task, purpose, and audience.

WHST.6-8.7 Conduct short research projects to answer a question (including a self-generated question), drawing on several sources and generating additional related, focused questions that allow for multiple avenues of exploration.

WHST.6-8.9 Draw evidence from informational texts to support analysis, reflection, and research.

ALASKA STATE STANDARDS FOR CULTURALLY RESPONSIVE SCHOOLS

C.A A culturally-responsive curriculum reinforces the integrity of the cultural knowledge that students bring with them.

C.B A culturally-responsive curriculum recognizes cultural knowledge as part of a living and constantly adapting system that is grounded in the past, but continues to grow through the present and into the future.

C.C A culturally-responsive curriculum uses the local language and cultural knowledge as a foundation for the rest of the curriculum.

C.D A culturally-responsive curriculum fosters a complementary relationship across knowledge derived from diverse knowledge systems.

C.E A culturally-responsive curriculum situates local knowledge and actions in a global context.

Teacher's Guide: Vocabulary

Aboriginal: The first people to inhabit a region. In the case of Alaska Natives, their aboriginal and ancestral presence in Alaska dates back thousands of years.

Civil Rights: The rights to individual personal freedom established by the U.S. Constitution, regardless of a person's sex, religion, or race, and guaranteed equal protection under the law. The First Amendment to the U.S. constitution protects a citizen's freedom of religion, speech, press, freedom of assembly, and freedom to petition the government. These guarantees are considered a cornerstone of our democracy.

Grumman Goose: A twin-engine, eight-seat, amphibious flying boat with a fuselage designed to land directly in water, like the hull of a boat, as opposed to more familiar floatplanes that rely on pontoons to keep the fuselage away from the water. The Grumman Goose was popular with the US Navy during WWII and, although not manufactured since 1945, is still used in some areas of Alaska. There are only about 30 airworthy Grumman Gooses in the world today.

House of Representatives: Article One of the U.S. Constitution specifies that two houses or chambers make up our federal legislature (the U.S. Congress). The upper house is the Senate and the lower house is the House of Representatives. Each body has different responsibilities and requirements. For example, only the House of Representatives can initiate revenue-raising bills or begin an impeachment process against a government official.

Indigenous: A term used to describe plants, animals and humans originating or occurring naturally in a particular region or environment.

Inequity: Lack of fairness and justice. Unequal treatment.

Iñupiaq: An Indigenous person of northern Alaska. The word means "real or genuine person." It also refers to their language. The collective term or plural is Iñupiat. [https://www.uaf.edu/anlc/languages/inupiaq.php]

Legislature: A legislature is an assembly of elected citizens with the authority to make laws for a political entity such as a country, state, or city. In many states in the U.S., the legislature is made up of two parts: a senate and a house of representatives. Members are typically elected to office for a specified term by popular vote. Legislatures and their power and use vary from country to country.

Mixed Breed: An offensive way to describe a person of mixed ancestry.

Prejudice: 1) Preconceived judgment or opinion. 2) An adverse opinion or leaning formed without just grounds or sufficient knowledge. [Merriam Webster]

Racism: 1) A belief that race is the primary determinant of human traits and capacities and that racial differences produce an inherent superiority of a particular race. 2) A political or social system founded on racism. [Merriam Webster]

Senate: The "upper" house or chamber in the US Congress and in every state legislature except Nebraska, which has only a single legislative chamber. Legislation cannot be enacted without the consent of both chambers. The Senate ratifies treaties, approves presidential appointments, and determines the outcome of an impeachment process.

Territory: A geographic area belonging to, or under the jurisdiction of, a governmental authority without the full rights of a state.

Please see Glossary definition of "territorial government."

Testimony: A true, formal, written or spoken statement based on personal experience or personal knowledge. Elizabeth Peratrovich presented formal testimony about her experience before a legislative body. In a court of law, testimony is more narrowly defined as evidence given by a witness who is required to tell the truth under oath or penalty of perjury.

Tlingit: Indigenous people of the Pacific Northwest Coast of North America. The name means "People of the Tides." They are one of three tribes to populate Southeast Alaska. The others are the Haida and the Tsimshian.

Tuberculosis: A highly infectious, bacterial disease characterized by the growth of nodules (tubercles) in the tissues, especially the lungs.

Unanimous: The agreement and consent of all.

Teacher's Guide: Map Key

Kichxáan (Ketchikan)

Juneau

Lawáak (Klawock)

Gánti Yaakw Séedi (Petersburg)

Deishú (Haines)

Wales

Nome

Deering

Aleutian Islands

Kéix' (Kake)

Tinaghu (Tenakee)

Sheet'ká (Sitka)

Maaxłakxaała (Metlakatla)

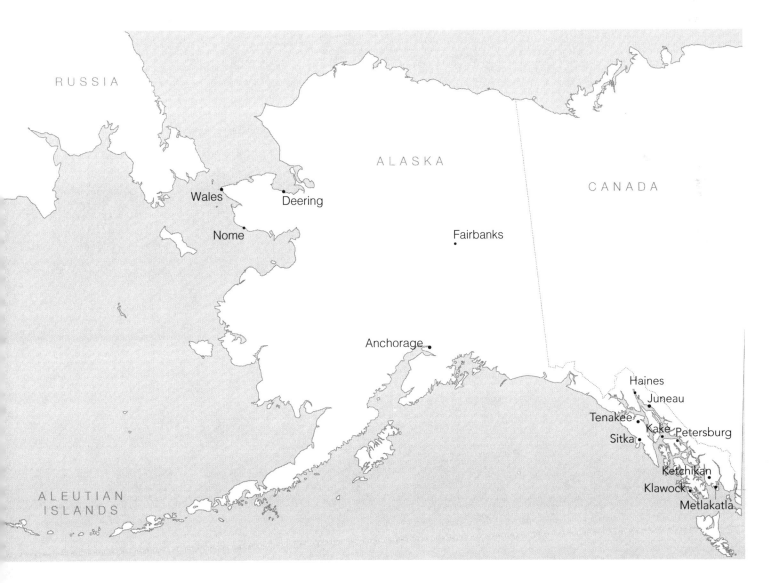

TEACHER'S GUIDE
RESPONSES

RESPONSES

1. Explains the history leading up to 1911, the year Elizabeth was born.

2. Roy Peratrovich Jr.'s introduction gives more authority to the book. There are no living contemporaries of Elizabeth. Roy is the only living child of Roy and Elizabeth Peratrovich, and has shared extensive memories, photos, and documents of his mother's life. Roy Jr.'s recollections help make the story more personal.

3. Elizabeth's friend Stella Martin called Elizabeth a "Fighter in Velvet Gloves." Roy Peratrovich Jr. explains how the description fit his mother well because no matter how great her fight for equality was, she always pursued it with grace and dignity.

4. The backdrop for Elizabeth's birth was in itself a poignant story. The introduction explains the cruelty that many Alaska Native people suffered at the hands of white explorers and settlers. It is a testament to Elizabeth's character that she was able to achieve so much, in spite of the inequality and prejudice so prevalent at the time.

5. One cannot separate oneself from one's birth. The circumstances of Elizabeth's birth are part of who she was as a person. And while adoption affects many people, not just Alaska Natives, tuberculosis was especially prevalent among Alaska Native families and still is today. Finally, it was not uncommon in the Tlingit culture for families to take in a child who was born into difficult circumstances.

6. Independent research on tuberculosis in Alaska Native people or Native Americans.

Teacher's Guide: Chapters 2 and 3

RESPONSES

1. Public speaking was especially important when Elizabeth was growing up because the Tlingit people did not have a long history of written language. Tlingit communication was an oral tradition until contact with white traders necessitated that words be transcribed onto paper. Today Tlingit and other traditional Alaska languages are both spoken and written, but many Alaska Native cultures continue to place a high value on storytelling and other oration skills.

2. The Alaska Native Brotherhood (ANB) was founded in 1912 in Sitka to advance Alaska Native rights throughout Southeast Alaska and to support improvements in educational opportunities, employment, social services, health services, and housing for all Alaska Native people. Elizabeth's adoptive father, Andrew Wanamaker, was a charter member and honorary founder. The ANB is now considered the oldest Indigenous civil rights organization in the world. The Alaska Native Sisterhood (ANS) was started in 1914. Both organizations were central to the battle for civil rights in Alaska. Today, the ANB and ANS remain important organizations and continue to pursue their original missions.

3. Reverend Sheldon Jackson visited Alaska in 1877 as a missionary and later worked successfully to fund and greatly expand the education system for Alaska Natives. Unfortunately, he also subscribed to the theory that schools should "civilize and assimilate" Alaska Natives into the White (historically European) culture. This meant forcing Alaska Native students to cut their hair, adopt Christianity, speak only English, and abandon their traditional customs and practices. While Jackson's approach brought useful skills and knowledge to many Alaska Native students, subsequent studies have identified serious adverse effects as well. Students felt they missed out on learning traditional skills and beliefs that were fundamental to their history, culture, and sense of who they are as people. When they returned to their villages, they felt they no longer belonged. And forcing families to allow their often very young children to attend distant schools was catastrophic for many communities. Traumas related to the boarding school experience have been linked to drug and alcohol abuse and suicide.

4. Elizabeth accompanied her dad, a lay-minister for the Presbyterian church, throughout Southeast Alaska on a boat he helped build. In every village, her dad preached at the local church, and Elizabeth sat in the back listening intently to every word. She later learned that if she spoke clearly and chose her words carefully, as her adoptive father had done, people really listened to her.

1. William Paul Sr. was a founding member of the Alaska Native Brotherhood and the first Alaska Native person to become an attorney in Alaska. He was also the first Alaska Native person to be elected to the Alaska Territorial House of Representatives, and the first to serve as an officer in the federal Bureau of Indian Affairs. He was very involved in the Alaska Native Claims Settlement Act of 1971.

2. The country was engulfed in the financial crisis of the Great Depression. There were no loans available, and Elizabeth and Roy couldn't afford to pay tuition. They returned to Klawock, but not before getting married in Bellingham, Washington.

3. Juneau was the capital of the Territory of Alaska. Because that is where the laws were made, Elizabeth thought she and Roy Sr. could do more for their people there.

4. See reference: "Statehood for Alaska: The Issues Involved and the Facts About the Issues" by George Sundborg. https://www.scribd.com/document/39931347/Statehood-for-Alaska-The-Issues-Involved-and-the-Facts-About-the-Issues

A territory generally has a territorial governor appointed by the Federal government. Alaska's territorial governor, Ernest Gruening, was appointed by President Franklin Delano Roosevelt in 1939.

The US currently has sixteen territories, including Puerto Rico, Guam, and the Virgin Islands. Most territories are governed by the US federal government, but the people who live there have no voting representation in Congress. Unlike most other territories, the Territory of Alaska was granted the full protection of the US Constitution and the right to establish its own territorial legislature. Alaska became a full-fledged state in 1959.

The First Organic Act was passed in 1884. It allowed Alaska to become a judicial district as well as a civil one, with an appointed governor, judges, clerks, marshals, and other federal officials. It wasn't until 1912 that Congress passed the Second Organic Act, which created the US Territory of Alaska and the territorial legislature. The territory included four judicial districts, each with twenty-four elected representatives and two senators. The first territorial legislature did not include a single Alaska Native.

1. Russians were the first white people to discover Alaska. In 1741, Vitus Bering, the Danish navigator of a Russian expedition, made the first sighting, which lead to many excursions into the new land and eventually Russian colonization. Unlike the American settlers who followed, the Russians allowed the Alaska Natives to speak their own languages and practice their traditional customs. Many Alaska Natives at that time learned to speak Russian in order to better communicate with the newcomers.

2. One of the reasons Governor Gruening was sympathetic to the anti-discrimination bill was that he was Jewish and had been the subject of discrimination himself. During and prior to WWII, there was a great deal of antisemitism in America. Gruening helped draft the first Alaska anti-discrimination bill and presented it to the Territorial Legislature in 1943. He tried, mostly unsuccessfully, to get local businesses to take down their racist signs.

3. President Franklin Delano Roosevelt was the United State's 32nd, and longest-serving President, elected for five consecutive terms from 1933-1945, leading the US through the Great Depression and World War II. His legs were paralyzed from polio but that didn't seem to slow him down. He appointed Ernest Gruening Governor of Territorial Alaska in 1939 and reappointed him twice.

4. In 1943, the anti-discrimination bill passed in the territorial house of representatives but was defeated in the senate. This was mostly because the legislature was dominated by white men who represented business interests outside Alaska. Equal treatment of Alaska Native people was not of interest to them and some likely viewed it as an impediment to their business activities.

5. In 1944, Alberta Schenk was a 17-year-old high school student in Nome. Her father was a white army veteran of WWI and her mother was an Alaska Native woman of Iñupiat descent. She worked at Nome's local movie theater which, like most theaters in Alaska, had segregated seating separating whites from Alaska Natives. She spoke out about the Dream Theater's unfair seating arrangement and was fired. In response, she wrote an essay

about the seating policy that appeared in the local paper, the Nome Nugget. Later, she and her date, a white army sergeant, sat in the "whites only" section. She was arrested and spent a night in jail. Her story spread throughout Alaska. Alberta later sent a telegram to Gov. Gruening telling him about the incident. The governor wired the mayor of Nome, Edward Anderson, demanding an explanation. The mayor replied that there would be no more similar incidents. (*Many Battles* by Ernest Gruening, p 321.) In 1945, Mayor Edward Anderson introduced the anti-discrimination bill in the House of Representatives. Alberta Schenck's aunt, Frances Longley, an ANS member in Nome, was also the longtime partner of Senator O.D. Cochran of Nome, an active supporter of the bill.

6. During her travels throughout Alaska, Elizabeth stressed the importance of the anti-discrimination bill, why it was important for Alaska Natives to vote, and why they should consider running for office. She also encouraged the establishment of many new ANB and ANS chapters.

7. The Toilet Paper Defense was the name given to a legal argument by William Paul Sr. in his court defense of a Tlingit Elder, Charlie Jones, who had been arrested for voting illegally. Attorney William Paul Sr. showed that even though Jones lived an Alaska Native lifestyle and spoke only Tlingit, he owned a home, paid taxes, used a knife and fork, and employed toilet paper and not tree leaves for personal hygiene. Since Mr. Jones lived like any other civilized person, Paul argued, he was entitled to the same privileges.

RESPONSES

1. Frank Peratrovich (Roy Sr.'s brother) of Klawock, Andrew Hope, a boat-builder from Sitka, and Percy Ipalook of Wales. After serving for a term in the House, Frank Peratrovich was elected to the Senate, where he eventually was voted president. The election of these Alaska Native lawmakers helped break up the stalemate in Alaska's Territorial Legislature. It forced legislators to pay attention to Alaska Natives and their concerns.

2. Shell Simmons: Please see Glossary p. 89-90.

RESPONSES

1. The bill was less likely to pass in the Senate because it was a smaller body with no Alaska Native members and some fierce opponents to the bill.

2. Senator O. Cochran of Nome and Senator Norman Ray "Doc" Walker of Ketchikan are the only ones mentioned in *Fighter in Velvet Gloves*, but the vote was 11–5, so there were nine others who also voted in favor.

3. Allen Shattuck of Juneau gave a speech about how he thought Alaska Natives were uncivilized savages. Frank Whaley of Fairbanks thought the bill would cause more lawsuits to enrich attorneys. He also said Alaska Natives smelled. Grenold Collins of Anchorage maintained the "mixed breed" was causing all the problems.

4. Roy Peratrovich Sr. testified about what it was like to be discriminated against in one's own homeland.

5. 19–5 in the House of Representatives and 11–5 in the Senate.

6. After signing the bill, Gov. Gruening gave the pen to Elizabeth and said, "This was the most important piece of legislation passed in Alaska and will help the most in its development. It never would have passed without your speech." (p.58).

7. As Alaska Natives, they previously had not been allowed there. Also, it must have been very affirming when they began dancing to have the others in the room form a circle around them.

8. Elizabeth Peratrovich helped abolish inequality in the Alaska juvenile code, worked with the ANS to promote public-health hospital services for Alaska Native people suffering from tuberculosis, and was successful in getting the local newspaper editor to handle all juvenile crime reports the same regardless of race.

9. Often people have preconceptions about race that are based on hearsay or incorrect information. Education and simply encouraging people of different backgrounds to live and work together and get to know each other can help correct that.

10. There is no right or wrong answer here, as long as it is thoughtful.

11. Elizabeth believed that if someone is confident about their own worth as a person, then they will not feel hurt by the ignorant words or actions of others.

12. The author doesn't really answer this question, but Elizabeth died in the Christian Science Care Facility in Seattle because she had no health insurance and couldn't afford hospital care.

13. She was 47 years old.

1. Governor Steve Cowper (pronounced C-o-o-per), proclaimed Elizabeth Peratrovich Day on April 20, 1988. The date for celebration was later changed to February 16, to coincide with the date the anti-discrimination bill was signed into law.

2. A bronze bust of Elizabeth Peratrovich is displayed in the Alaska State Capitol. A replica of that bust is displayed at the National Museum of the American Indian. Finally, The Flight of the Raven, a bronze sculpture created by Roy Peratrovich Jr. may be seen in the Roy and Elizabeth Peratrovich Park in downtown Anchorage. "Roy Jr explained that his sculpture was a futuristic totem pole, a reminder of how his parents helped Alaska soar to new heights." P 72.

3. The U.S. Mint released a commemorative silver dollar coin featuring Elizabeth Peratrovich's likeness in February, 2020.

4. Elizabeth and Roy Peratrovich Sr. are buried side by side in the Evergreen Cemetery in Juneau, Alaska.

5. Yes, especially since the author is a native Alaskan but not an Alaska Native. Her personal knowledge of and connection to many of the people who knew Elizabeth or were involved in the passage of the anti-discrimination bill gave her a unique perspective.

6. There is no right or wrong answer to this question.

About the Author
Annie Boochever

Annie Boochever grew up in Juneau when Alaska was still a territory. Racism, although subtler than before passage of the anti-discrimination bill, was still pervasive. Even as a child, she was painfully aware of it.

After a career teaching music, theater, library and high school English, Annie earned an MFA in Creative Writing for Children and Young Adults. Her first book, *Bristol Bay Summer* (Alaska Northwest Books, 2014), was an Alaska State Battle of the Book's pick for middle-grades and an International Literary Classic's winner for best first novel.

Retired from teaching, when Annie is not writing, she loves spending time with her grandchildren. She recently moved to Bellingham, Washington where she lives with her husband and Dutch dog Zz.

Ready for an adventure: Annie Boochever in her son Zach's boat with Zz. *Photo courtesy of Annie Boochever.*

About the Son
Roy Peratrovich Jr.

ELIZABETH'S LAST LIVING CHILD

As of this writing, Roy Peratrovich Jr. is eighty-six-years old. He is the last living child of Elizabeth and Roy Peratrovich Sr. The first Alaska Native certified as a civil engineer in Alaska, Roy Jr. cofounded the engineering firm Peratrovich, Nottingham, and Drage.

Peratrovich is also a successful artist and has created sculptures honoring his mother and father which can be found in parks, buildings, and museums in Alaska and Washington, DC. He is also the illustrator and author of the book *Little Whale: A Story of the Last Tlingit War Canoe*. Peratrovich collaborated with Boochever on *Fighter in Velvet Gloves* by providing documentation and stories about his mother, as well as historical photos from his family collection.

Annie Boochever with Roy Peratrovich Jr., 2015. *Photographed by Roy's wife, Toby Peratrovich, in their backyard.*